SACRED SPACE

from the website www.sacredspace.ie

Prayer from the Irish Jesuits

LOYOLA PRESS.
A JESUIT MINISTRY
Chicago

LOYOLAPRESS.
A JESUIT MINISTRY

3441 N. Ashland Avenue
Chicago, Illinois 60657
(800) 621-1008
www.loyolapress.com

Scripture quotations are from the *New Revised Standard Version Bible: Catholic Edition*, copyright © 1989, 1993 National Council of the Churches of Christ in the United States of America. Used by permission. All rights reserved.

Cover art credit: © iStock/Qweek

ISBN-13: 978-0-8294-4450-6
ISBN-10: 0-8294-4450-5

16 17 18 19 20 21 Versa 10 9 8 7 6 5 4 3 2 1

Contents

The Presence of God

Bless all who worship you, almighty God,
from the rising of the sun to its setting:
from your goodness enrich us,
by your love inspire us,
by your Spirit guide us,
by your power protect us,
in your mercy receive us,
now and always.

How to Use This Booklet

During each week of Lent, begin by reading the "Something to think and pray about each day this week." Then proceed through "The Presence of God," "Freedom," and "Consciousness" steps to prepare yourself to hear the Word of God in your heart. In the next step, "The Word," turn to the Scripture reading for each day of the week. Inspiration points are provided if you need them. Then return to the "Conversation" and "Conclusion" steps. Follow this process every day of Lent.

March 1—March 4

Something to think and pray about each day this week:

Desired into Existence

I maintain that God—out of the abundance of divine relational life, not any need for us—desires humans into existence for the sake of friendship. This thesis may sound strange, because it runs counter to much teaching about God. To be honest, I questioned it myself when I first began to think it through. But over the years, as my own relationship with God has deepened and I have listened to people talk about how God relates to them, I have become convinced that the best analogy for the relationship God wants with us is friendship.

—William A. Barry, SJ, *Lenten Meditations*

The Presence of God
To be present is to arrive as one is and open up to the other.
At this instant, as I arrive here, God is present waiting for me.
God always arrives before me, desiring to connect with me
even more than my most intimate friend.
I take a moment and greet my loving God.

Freedom
I am free. When I look at these words in writing, they seem to create in me a feeling of awe. Yes, a wonderful feeling of freedom. Thank you, God.

Consciousness
To be conscious about something is to be aware of it. Dear Lord, help me to remember that you gave me life. Thank you for the gift of life.
Teach me to slow down, to be still and enjoy the pleasures created for me. To be aware of the beauty that surrounds me. The marvel of mountains, the calmness of lakes, the fragility of a flower petal. I need to remember that all these things come from you.

The Word
The Word of God comes to us through the Scriptures. May the Holy Spirit enlighten my mind and heart to respond to the Gospel teachings. (Please turn to the Scripture on the following pages. Inspiration points are there should you need them. When you are ready, return here to continue.)

Conversation
I begin to talk to Jesus about the piece of Scripture I have just read. What part of it strikes a chord in me? Perhaps the words of a friend—or some story I have heard recently—will slowly rise to the surface in my consciousness. If so, does the story throw light on what the Scripture passage may be trying to say to me?

Conclusion
Glory be to the Father, and to the Son, and to the Holy Spirit,
As it was in the beginning, is now and ever shall be,
World without end. Amen.

Wednesday 1st March
Ash Wednesday

Matthew 6:1–6, 16–18

Jesus said, "Beware of practicing your piety before others in order to be seen by them; for then you have no reward from your Father in heaven. So whenever you give alms, do not sound a trumpet before you, as the hypocrites do in the synagogues and in the streets, so that they may be praised by others. Truly I tell you, they have received their reward. But when you give alms, do not let your left hand know what your right hand is doing, so that your alms may be done in secret; and your Father who sees in secret will reward you. And whenever you pray, do not be like the hypocrites; for they love to stand and pray in the synagogues and at the street corners, so that they may be seen by others. Truly I tell you, they have received their reward. But whenever you pray, go into your room and shut the door and pray to your Father who is in secret; and your Father who sees in secret will reward you. . . . And whenever you fast, do not look dismal, like the hypocrites, for they disfigure their faces so as to show others that they are fasting. Truly I tell you, they have received their reward. But when you fast, put oil on your head and wash your face, so that your fasting may be seen not by others but by your Father who is in secret; and your Father who sees in secret will reward you."

- At this time of year, the church invites us to test our inner freedom—concerning food and drink, pornography, complaining, gossiping, and so on. What habits make you hard to live with? Lent is about regaining control of our own lives, especially in those areas that damage other people.

- Do I have a secret room in which I meet God? Am I happy to have God see all that I do? The kingdom of God becomes visible through my public religious practices and also through my private works of charity and acts of faith.

Thursday 2nd March
Luke 9:22–25

Jesus said to his disciples, "The Son of Man must undergo great suffering, and be rejected by the elders, chief priests, and scribes, and be killed, and on the third day be raised." Then he said to them all, "If any want to become my followers, let them deny themselves and take up their cross daily and follow me. For those who want to save their life will lose it, and those who lose their life for my sake will save it. What does it profit them if they gain the whole world, but lose or forfeit themselves?"

- *Deny yourself and take up your cross daily.* Lord, I used to think this meant looking for mortifications. You have taught me that my cross is myself, my ego, the pains in my body, my awkwardness, my mistakes. To follow you is to move beyond ego trips. It means coping with the business of life without trampling on others or making them suffer.

- The Gospel is unambiguous: suffering and self-displacement are the hallmarks of a disciple. Jesus goes the way of the cross. He does not hoard his life, even though living must have had a special quality for him. I am called not to hoard my life but to live generously.

Friday 3rd March
Matthew 9:14–15

Then the disciples of John came to him, saying, "Why do we and the Pharisees fast often, but your disciples do not fast?" And Jesus said to them, "The wedding guests cannot mourn as long as the bridegroom is with them, can they? The days will come when the bridegroom is taken away from them, and then they will fast."

- Spend some time each day allowing the joy of God to fill your heart. Spend some time mourning with him, as joy is lost for so many. Any fasting is to remind us that the Lord of all joy suffers in his people, perhaps in people who are near to us. Prayer brings us near to others and near to God.

- Here Jesus uses the notion of fasting to reveal that the God whom the Jews hunger for has arrived. Rejoicing, not mourning, is the appropriate response to the presence of divine mercy revealed in Jesus. Lord, this Lent may my prayer and my fasting reveal my inner hunger for you.

Saturday 4th March
Luke 5:27–32

After this Jesus went out and saw a tax collector named Levi, sitting at the tax booth; and he said to him, "Follow me." And he got up, left everything, and followed him. Then Levi gave a great banquet for him in his house; and there was a large crowd of tax collectors and others sitting at the table with them. The Pharisees and their scribes were complaining to his disciples, saying, "Why do you eat and drink with tax collectors and sinners?" Jesus answered, "Those who are well have no need of a physician, but those who are sick; I have come to call not the righteous but sinners to repentance."

- Whom Jesus eats and drinks with is a distraction from what his mission is—to call us into a change of life. When we are focused on Jesus, we can eat and drink with anyone. We can invite anyone into our prayer and allow prayer to be a time of healing and forgiveness.

- Where are the Levis in my world? The drug push-
  ers, greedy CEOs, abusers, rapists, those who
  cheat on taxes or social welfare. Lord, these are the
  sick who need you as physician. How can I help
  you reach out to them?

The First Week of Lent
March 5—March 11

Something to think and pray about each day this week:

Truth and Discernment

It's difficult to make a good decision when you don't have all the information. It's also difficult to move forward while trying to deny part of your reality. Jesus came from a tradition that was brutally honest; just read a bit from any of Israel's prophets to see how forcefully they spoke the truth. Jesus continued in this vein as he talked about what it really took to be people of God, to participate in the kingdom of God. Jesus knew what John the Baptist knew before him and what the prophets knew before both of them: without truth, people cannot heal. If we ignore the root cause of our wounds, we will continue to be wounded, even if we heal some of the damage. We might fix what has been harmed. But if we continue doing what caused the harm in the first place, we will simply acquire (or inflict) new wounds because the core activity has not changed.

Lent is a good time to stop our activity long enough to look at it carefully, prayerfully, and to determine the specific truths of the situation.

—Vinita Hampton Wright, *Praying Freedom*

The Presence of God
Be still and know that I am God. Lord, may your spirit guide me to seek your loving presence more and more. For it is there I find rest and refreshment from this busy world.

Freedom
By God's grace I was born to live in freedom. Free to enjoy the pleasures he created for me. Dear Lord, grant that I may live as you intended, with complete confidence in your loving care.

Consciousness
In God's loving presence I unwind the past day, starting from now and looking back, moment by moment.
I gather in all the goodness and light, in gratitude.
I attend to the shadows and what they say to me, seeking healing, courage, forgiveness.

The Word
The Word of God comes to us through the Scriptures. May the Holy Spirit enlighten my mind and heart to respond to the Gospel teachings. (Please turn to the Scripture on the following pages. Inspiration points are there should you need them. When you are ready, return here to continue.)

Conversation

Jesus, you always welcomed little children when you walked on this earth. Teach me to have a childlike trust in you. To live in the knowledge that you will never abandon me.

Conclusion

Glory be to the Father, and to the Son, and to the Holy Spirit,
As it was in the beginning, is now and ever shall be,
World without end. Amen.

Sunday 5th March
First Sunday of Lent
Matthew 4:1–11

Then Jesus was led up by the Spirit into the wilderness to be tempted by the devil. He fasted for forty days and forty nights, and afterwards he was famished. The tempter came and said to him, "If you are the Son of God, command these stones to become loaves of bread." But he answered, "It is written, 'One does not live by bread alone, but by every word that comes from the mouth of God.'"

- Our real hungers are fed by the meaning and the love of the Word of God. One form of prayer is to allow ourselves to be addressed in the heart by the Word of God. Let a phrase or word from this passage of Scripture echo in your mind today.

- That Jesus was tempted meant that he truly desired what the devil offered him. Of course he was hungry. His body desired what it needed. In what ways might the devil use my legitimate, real desires to lead me astray? Open my eyes, Lord, so that I can recognize temptation when it comes.

Monday 6th March
Matthew 25:31–46

Jesus said to his disciples, "When the Son of Man comes in his glory, and all the angels with him, then he will sit on the throne of his glory. All the nations will be gathered before him, and he will separate people one from another as a shepherd separates the sheep from the goats, and he will put the sheep at his right hand and the goats at the left. Then the king will say to those at his right hand, 'Come, you that are blessed by my Father, inherit the kingdom prepared for you from the foundation of the world; for I was hungry and you gave me food, I was thirsty and you gave me something to drink, I was a stranger and you welcomed me, I was naked and you gave me clothing, I was sick and you took care of me, I was in prison and you visited me.' Then the righteous will answer him, 'Lord, when was it that we saw you hungry and gave you food, or thirsty and gave you something to drink? And when was it that we saw you a stranger and welcomed you, or naked and gave you clothing? And when was it that we saw you sick or in prison and visited you?' And the king will answer them, 'Truly I tell you, just as you did it to one of the least of these who are members of my family, you did it to me.' Then he will say to those at his left hand, 'You that are accursed, depart from me into the eternal fire prepared for the devil and his angels; for I was hungry and you gave me no food, I was thirsty and you gave me nothing to drink, I was a stranger and you did not welcome me, naked and you did not give me clothing, sick and in prison and you did not visit me.' Then they also will answer, 'Lord, when was it that we saw you hungry or thirsty or a stranger or naked or sick or in prison, and did not take care of you?' Then he will answer them, 'Truly I tell you, just as you did not do it to one of the least of these, you did not do it to me. And these will go away into eternal punishment, but the righteous into eternal life.'"

- This message is simple, Lord. You will judge me on my love for and service to others. You are there in the poor, the sick, the prisoners, the strangers. May I recognize your face.

- The story does not use fancy words about justice and solidarity but speaks of food, clothing, something to drink, protection from elements. What matters is not a theoretical love but compassion that helps the person in need.

Tuesday 7th March
Matthew 6:7–15

Jesus said, "When you are praying, do not heap up empty phrases as the Gentiles do; for they think that they will be heard because of their many words. Do not be like them, for your Father knows what you need before you ask him. Pray then in this way: Our Father in heaven, hallowed be your name. Your kingdom come. Your will be done, on earth as it is in heaven. Give us this day our daily bread. And forgive us our debts, as we also have forgiven our debtors. And do not bring us to the time of trial, but rescue us from the evil one. For if you forgive others their trespasses, your heavenly Father will also forgive you; but if you do not forgive others, neither will your Father forgive your trespasses."

- This simple prayer that Jesus taught is as new and fresh today as when it was first spoken. It reveals how things are to be between God and ourselves, and also with one another. Let me slowly say the Our Father, as if I were praying it for the first time.

- Jesus calls his disciples to pray and teaches them how. Prayer, he says, is not a magic formula but a trusting relationship between God and myself. The Our Father invites me to simplicity and sincerity of heart. It expresses an attitude of complete dependency on God. Jesus, the petitions in this prayer put God at the center of everything. That is how you lived. Help me do the same.

Wednesday 8th March
Luke 11:29–32

When the crowds were increasing, Jesus began to say, "This generation is an evil generation; it asks for a sign, but no sign will be given to it except the sign of Jonah. For just as Jonah became a sign to the people of Nineveh, so the Son of Man will be to this generation. The queen of the South will rise at the judgment with the people of this generation and condemn them, because she came from the ends of the earth to listen to the wisdom of Solomon, and see, something greater than Solomon is here! The people of Nineveh will rise up at the judgment with this generation and condemn it, because they repented at the proclamation of Jonah, and see, something greater than Jonah is here!"

- Jonah converted the great city of Nineveh by his godliness and his preaching, not by miracles. Holiness is a greater marvel than special effects but less easily recognized. Lord, your hand is more evident in saintliness than in extraordinary signs. Open my eyes to your work in my sisters and brothers.

- Jesus, you stand before me as a sign. Like Jonah, you are swallowed up by death, but you rise from the dead and challenge me to walk in newness of life. Stay with me in my times of blindness and usher me back into your saving presence.

Thursday 9th March
Matthew 7:7–12

Jesus said, "Ask, and it will be given to you; search, and you will find; knock, and the door will be opened for you. For everyone who asks receives, and everyone who searches finds, and for everyone who knocks, the door will be opened. Is there anyone among you who, if your child asks for bread, will give a stone? Or if the child asks for a fish, will give a snake? If you then, who are evil, know how to give good gifts to your children, how much more will your Father in heaven give good things to those who ask him! In everything do to others as you would have them do to you; for this is the law and the prophets."

- In the very act of praying we receive something from God. As we open our hearts to God in prayer, God's hands are open to give us good gifts. We leave a time of prayer with an increase of faith, hope, and love, which is the consolation of God.

- Parent/child is only a metaphor for what happens in prayer. I know, Lord, that you always hear my cry, but I do not always understand your answer. I will still go on praying to you, happy to fall back on the "Our Father."

Friday 10th March
Matthew 5:20–26

Jesus said, "For I tell you, unless your righteousness exceeds that of the scribes and Pharisees, you will never enter the kingdom of heaven. You have heard that it was said to those of ancient times, 'You shall not murder; and whoever murders shall be liable to judgment.' But I say to you that if you are angry with a brother or sister, you will be liable to judgment; and if you insult a brother or sister, you will be liable to the council; and if you say, 'You fool,' you will be liable to the hell of fire. So when you are offering your gift at the altar, if you remember that your brother or sister has something against you, leave your gift there before the altar and go; first be reconciled to your brother or sister, and then come and offer your gift. Come to terms quickly with your accuser while you are on the way to court with him, or your accuser may hand you over to the judge, and the judge to the guard, and you will be thrown into prison. Truly I tell you, you will never get out until you have paid the last penny."

- Lord, you are pushing my conscience inward. I will be judged not just by what I have done on the exterior but also by the voluntary movements of my heart. God sees the heart and sees how far I go along with hatred, lust, or pride. I should be responding more to God's gaze than to anyone else's.

- Jesus is unhappy with taking the prohibition of murder too literally or restrictively. He wants it to include any kind of psychological or verbal abuse of another human being. Life is meant to be about relationships that are peaceful and harmonious.

Hence the need for reconciliation when relationships break down. Am I in need of reconciliation with anyone today?

Saturday 11th March
Matthew 5:43–48

Jesus said to the disciples, "You have heard that it was said, 'You shall love your neighbor and hate your enemy.' But I say to you, Love your enemies and pray for those who persecute you, so that you may be children of your Father in heaven; for he makes his sun rise on the evil and on the good, and sends rain on the righteous and on the unrighteous. For if you love those who love you, what reward do you have? Do not even the tax collectors do the same? And if you greet only your brothers and sisters, what more are you doing than others? Do not even the Gentiles do the same? Be perfect, therefore, as your heavenly Father is perfect."

• Jesus emphasizes that the easy option is not the correct one. How simple to love and be happy with those who love you! But the kingdom of God is much bigger than that: You must love all. Lord, you call us out of our comfort zones. Our growth is measured by the breadth of our love. Help us grow in love!

- Loving our enemies is among the most challenging precepts taught by Jesus. Notice how he finds motivation and a standard in the love shown by our Father in heaven—a love that is all-embracing, nondiscriminating, inclusive. Ponder how Jesus himself modeled this love. Do I want to live and love like him?

The Second Week of Lent
March 12—March 18

Something to think and pray about each day this week:

The Communal Journey

Lent is indeed how God draws us home as individuals, but it is also a very communal journey. We never journey alone, no matter how lonely we may feel. We are always journeying together. If we can experience our journey in communion with others, it makes it so much clearer that we are on a journey together. When we can share our experiences with a close friend or our worship community, we can enjoy support that allows grace to flourish. Let us pray for one another on this journey, especially for those who need and desire a change of heart on this pilgrimage to Easter joy. Choosing and acting Lent are so important because we are body-persons. We experience things with our senses, relish them with our imaginations, and we share in God's own creative and loving activity when our hearts and hands work together for and with others.

—Andy Alexander, SJ, and Maureen McCann Waldron, *Praying Lent*

The Presence of God

I pause for a moment and think of the love and the grace that God showers on me: I am created in the image and likeness of God; I am God's dwelling place.

Freedom

Lord, you created me to live in freedom. May your Holy Spirit guide me to follow you freely. Instill in my heart a desire to know and love you more each day.

Consciousness

How am I really feeling? Lighthearted? Heavyhearted?
I may be very much at peace, happy to be here.
Equally, I may be frustrated, worried, or angry.
I acknowledge how I really am. It is the real me that the Lord loves.

The Word

I read the Word of God slowly, a few times over, and I listen to what God is saying to me. (Please turn to the Scripture on the following pages. Inspiration points are there should you need them. When you are ready, return here to continue.)

Conversation

I know with certainty there were times when you carried me, Lord. When it was through your strength I got through the dark times in my life.

Conclusion

I thank God for these moments we have spent together and for any insights I have been given concerning the text.

Sunday 12th March
The Second Sunday of Lent
Matthew 17:1–9

Six days later, Jesus took with him Peter and James and his brother John and led them up a high mountain, by themselves. And he was transfigured before them, and his face shone like the sun, and his clothes became dazzling white. Suddenly there appeared to them Moses and Elijah, talking with him. Then Peter said to Jesus, "Lord, it is good for us to be here; if you wish, I will make three dwellings here, one for you, one for Moses, and one for Elijah." While he was still speaking, suddenly a bright cloud overshadowed them, and from the cloud a voice said, "This is my Son, the Beloved; with him I am well pleased; listen to him!" When the disciples heard this, they fell to the ground and were overcome by fear. But Jesus came and touched them, saying, "Get up and do not be afraid." And when they looked up, they saw no one except Jesus himself alone. As they were coming down the mountain, Jesus ordered them, "Tell no one about the vision until after the Son of Man has been raised from the dead."

- The disciples were privileged to see Jesus in glory, to recognize that their friend could be fully present to them and to God. Jesus saw that the experience was too much for them and told them to keep it in their hearts as they headed back toward the everyday. I thank God for the inspiration and encouragement I discover in my prayer and ask that I may know how best to carry it into everyday life.

- A listening heart is a heart warmed by the love of God and taught by his words. Prayer is better described as listening than speaking. Spend some time echoing his words, or just listening to the mood of love and peace in prayer.

Monday 13th March
Luke 6:36–38

Jesus said to the disciples, "Be merciful, just as your Father is merciful. Do not judge, and you will not be judged; do not condemn, and you will not be condemned. Forgive, and you will be forgiven; give, and it will be given to you. A good measure, pressed down, shaken together, running over, will be put into your lap; for the measure you give will be the measure you get back."

- What a beautiful, challenging Lenten program! Let us strive each day for the remainder of Lent not to judge or condemn; to forgive and tell others that they are forgiven; and to do one daily act of generosity. What transformed people we will be by Easter!

- Jesus stresses once again the primary importance
  of good relationships with others. The world
  would be a different place if we were merciful and
  non-condemning. Lord, my poor heart is very
  small, and it can also be very hard. Your heart
  is large and also very tender and compassionate.
  When I try to forgive others, my heart becomes a
  bit more like yours, and you swamp me with your
  overflowing generosity.

Tuesday 14th March
Matthew 23:1–12

Then Jesus said to the crowds and to his disciples,
"The scribes and the Pharisees sit on Moses' seat;
therefore, do whatever they teach you and follow it;
but do not do as they do, for they do not practice
what they teach. They tie up heavy burdens, hard to
bear, and lay them on the shoulders of others; but
they themselves are unwilling to lift a finger to move
them. They do all their deeds to be seen by others; for
they make their phylacteries broad and their fringes
long. They love to have the place of honor at ban-
quets and the best seats in the synagogues, and to be
greeted with respect in the marketplaces, and to have
people call them rabbi. But you are not to be called
rabbi, for you have one teacher, and you are all stu-
dents. And call no one your father on earth, for you

have one Father—the one in heaven. Nor are you to be called instructors, for you have one instructor, the Messiah. The greatest among you will be your servant. All who exalt themselves will be humbled, and all who humble themselves will be exalted."

- In the mysterious way that Scripture works, I am growing daily in knowledge of God's ways. You, Lord, are my teacher. I remember in prayer a moment when I felt humbled as I served somebody or did something really relevant for them. I offer this memory to God in thanks.

- Jesus does not take issue with how the Pharisees live, but he sees how they have become distracted from God by using human measures and assessments. Could it be that I am sometimes misled by wanting my way, by trying too hard to measure my own worth?

Wednesday 15th March
Matthew 20:17–28

While Jesus was going up to Jerusalem, he took the twelve disciples aside by themselves, and said to them on the way, "See, we are going up to Jerusalem, and the Son of Man will be handed over to the chief priests and scribes, and they will condemn him to death; then they will hand him over to the Gentiles to be mocked and flogged and crucified; and on the third day he will be raised." Then the mother of the sons of Zebedee came to him with her sons, and kneeling before him, she asked a favor of him. And he said to her, "What do you want?" She said to him, "Declare that these two sons of mine will sit, one at your right hand and one at your left, in your kingdom." But Jesus answered, "You do not know what you are asking. Are you able to drink the cup that I am about to drink?" They said to him, "We are able." He said to them, "You will indeed drink my cup, but to sit at my right hand and at my left, this is not mine to grant, but it is for those for whom it has been prepared by my Father." When the ten heard it, they were angry with the two brothers. But Jesus called them to him and said, "You know that the rulers of the Gentiles lord it over them, and their great ones are tyrants over them. It will not be so among you; but whoever wishes to be great among you must be your servant, and whoever wishes to be first among you must be your slave; just as the Son of Man came not to be served but to serve, and to give his life as a ransom for many."

- Jesus describes vividly the degrading ways in which he will be treated in his Passion. He does this to strengthen his disciples. When we decide to act lovingly in all we do, we become vulnerable. People will take advantage of us. But love will have the final word. We will be raised up as Jesus was. I thank God for this.

- Jesus, you abhor all forms of domination. The kingdom of God is to be a domination-free community. I can see how Christian churches fall into the trap of domination. But do I dominate anyone? Even in an argument? Do I even think I am better than anyone else?

Thursday 16th March
Luke 16:19–31

Jesus said to the Pharisees, "There was a rich man who was dressed in purple and fine linen and who feasted sumptuously every day. And at his gate lay a poor man named Lazarus, covered with sores, who longed to satisfy his hunger with what fell from the rich man's table; even the dogs would come and lick his sores. The poor man died and was carried away by the angels to be with Abraham. The rich man also died and was buried. In Hades, where he was being tormented, he looked up and saw Abraham far away with Lazarus by his side. He called out, 'Father Abraham, have mercy on me, and send Lazarus to dip the tip of his finger in water and cool my tongue; for I am in agony in these flames.' But Abraham said, 'Child, remember that during your lifetime you received your good things, and Lazarus in like manner evil things; but now he is comforted here, and you are in agony. Besides all this, between you and us a great chasm has been fixed, so that those who might want to pass from here to you cannot do so, and no one can cross from there to us.' He said, 'Then, father, I beg you to send him to my father's house—for I have five brothers—that he may warn them, so that they will not also come into this place of torment.' Abraham replied, 'They have Moses and the prophets; they should listen to them.' He said, 'No, father Abraham; but if someone goes to them from the dead, they will repent.' He said to him, 'If they do not listen to Moses and the prophets, neither will they be convinced even if someone rises from the dead.'"

- The poor are brought straight into the kingdom of God, while the rich have to endure the pain of conversion. I ponder the mysterious workings of God's providence. I pray for the rich that they be converted, and I ask to be shown how to share my own possessions with the needy.

- During Lent I try to hear the call to come back home to God. I join the great pilgrimage of people who, through the ages, have been called by Moses and the prophets to listen to the word of the Lord.

Friday 17th March
Matthew 21:33–43, 45–46

Jesus said, "Listen to another parable. There was a landowner who planted a vineyard, put a fence around it, dug a wine press in it, and built a watchtower. Then he leased it to tenants and went to another country. When the harvest time had come, he sent his slaves to the tenants to collect his produce. But the tenants seized his slaves and beat one, killed another, and stoned another. Again he sent other slaves, more than the first; and they treated them in the same way. Finally he sent his son to them, saying, 'They will respect my son.' But when the tenants saw the son, they said to themselves, 'This is the heir; come, let us kill him and get his inheritance. So they seized him, threw him out of the vineyard, and killed him. Now when the owner of the vineyard comes, what will he do to those tenants?" They said to him, "He will put those wretches to a miserable death, and lease the vineyard to other tenants who will give him the produce at the harvest time." Jesus said to them, "Have you never read in the Scriptures: 'The stone that the builders rejected has become the cornerstone; this was the Lord's doing, and it is amazing in our eyes'? Therefore I tell you, the kingdom of God will be taken away from you and given to a people that produces the fruits of the kingdom." . . . When the chief priests and the Pharisees heard his parables, they realized that he was speaking about them. They wanted to arrest him, but they feared the crowds, because they regarded him as a prophet.

- We are the tenants in the parable. God provides everything we need to make our vineyard prosper. God gives us the freedom to run the vineyard as we choose—but it is God's. This is what prayer is about—coming to know the mind of God about our lives. What fruits will I produce for the Lord?

- One of the saddest statements in the Gospels is this innocent comment by the father: "They will respect my son." I am frightened to think what would happen if Jesus came into our world today. His message about the kingdom of God would put him in direct opposition to so many other kingdoms. He would become an enemy to be got rid of. Jesus, you were thrown out and killed. But you took no revenge. Instead, by your love you reconciled everyone with God. May I always wish others well and pray for them, even if they hurt me.

Saturday 18th March
Luke 15:1–3, 11–32

Now all the tax collectors and sinners were coming near to listen to him. And the Pharisees and the scribes were grumbling and saying, "This fellow welcomes sinners and eats with them." So he told them this parable: . . . "There was a man who had two sons. The younger of them said to his father, 'Father, give me the share of the property that will belong to me.' So he divided his property between them. A few days later the younger son gathered all he had and traveled to a distant country, and there he squandered his property in dissolute living. When he had spent everything, a severe famine took place throughout that country, and he began to be in need. So he went and hired himself out to one of the citizens of that country, who sent him to his fields to feed the pigs. He would gladly have filled himself with the pods that the pigs were eating; and no one gave him anything. But when he came to himself he said, 'How many of my father's hired hands have bread enough and to spare, but here I am dying of hunger! I will get up and go to my father, and I will say to him, "Father, I have sinned against heaven and before you; I am no longer worthy to be called your son; treat me like one of your hired hands." So he set off and went to his father. But while he was still far off, his father saw him and was filled with compassion; he ran and put his arms around him and kissed him. Then the son said to him, 'Father, I have sinned against heaven and before you; I am no longer worthy to be called your son.' But the father said to his slaves, 'Quickly, bring out a robe—the best one—and put it on him; put a ring on his finger and sandals on his feet. And get the fatted calf and kill it, and let us eat and celebrate; for this son of mine was dead and is alive again; he was lost and is found!' And they began to celebrate. Now his elder son was in the field; and when he came and approached the house, he heard music and dancing. He called one of the slaves and asked what was going on. He replied, 'Your brother has come, and your father has killed the fatted calf, because he has got him back safe and sound.' Then he became angry and refused to go in. His father came out and began to plead with him. But he answered his father, 'Listen! For all these years I have been working like a slave for you, and I have never disobeyed your command; yet you have never given me even a young goat so that I might celebrate with my friends. But when this son of yours came back, who has devoured your property with prostitutes, you killed the fatted calf for him!' Then the father said to him, 'Son, you are always with me, and all that is mine is yours. But we had to celebrate and rejoice, because this brother of yours was dead and has come to life; he was lost and has been found.'"

- Jesus told a rather elaborate story. If you could not use a story but had to create a rational argument, how would you explain what Jesus was trying to say?

- Jesus, remind me that I am part of the eternal sacred story. And teach me how to communicate to others that their individual stories are also sacred.

The Third Week of Lent
March 19—March 25

Something to think and pray about each day this week:

Friendship Characteristics

It might help your reflection on friendship with God to think about your friendships with others. Who are your friends? What makes you say that they are your friends? You tell them things about yourself that you would not tell a stranger. You know that they will not tell others the secrets you share with them, that they will not hold against you what you tell them or hold it over your head as a threat. At the deepest level, you trust that they will remain your friends even when they know some of the less savory aspects of your past life and your character. You also trust that they will stick with you through thick and thin, through good times and tough times. And at least some of these characteristics will also be true of the relationship God wants with you. *What is the most important characteristic I look for in a friend? Can I also find this characteristic in my friendship with God?*

—William A. Barry, SJ, *Lenten Meditations*

The Presence of God
Jesus, help me be fully alive to your Holy Presence. Enfold me in your love. Let my heart become one with yours.

Freedom
I will ask God's help,
to be free from my own preoccupations,
to be open to God in this time of prayer,
to come to know, love, and serve God more.

Consciousness
I ask how I am within myself today? Am I particularly tired, stressed, or off form? If any of these characteristics apply, can I try to let go of the concerns that disturb me?

The Word
God speaks to each of us individually. I listen attentively to hear what God is saying to me. Read the text a few times, then listen. (Please turn to the Scripture on the following pages. Inspiration points are there should you need them. When you are ready, return here to continue.)

Conversation

Sometimes I wonder what I might say if I were to meet you in person, Lord.

I think I might say, Thank you, Lord, for always being there for me.

Conclusion

Glory be to the Father, and to the Son, and to the Holy Spirit,

As it was in the beginning, is now and ever shall be, World without end. Amen.

Sunday 19th March
Third Sunday of Lent
John 4:5–15, 19b–26, 39a, 40–42

So Jesus came to a Samaritan city called Sychar, near the plot of ground that Jacob had given to his son Joseph. Jacob's well was there, and Jesus, tired out by his journey, was sitting by the well. It was about noon. A Samaritan woman came to draw water, and Jesus said to her, "Give me a drink." (His disciples had gone to the city to buy food.) The Samaritan woman said to him, "How is it that you, a Jew, ask a drink of me, a woman of Samaria?" (Jews do not share things in common with Samaritans.) Jesus answered her, "If you knew the gift of God, and who it is that is saying to you, 'Give me a drink,' you would have asked him, and he would have given you living water." The woman said to him, "Sir, you have no bucket, and the well is deep. Where do you get that living water? Are you greater than our ancestor Jacob, who gave us the well, and with his sons and his flocks drank from it?" Jesus said to her, "Everyone who drinks of this water will be thirsty again, but those who drink of the water that I will give them will never be thirsty. The water that I will give will become in them a spring of water gushing up to eternal life." The woman said to him, "Sir, give me this water, so that I may never be thirsty or have to keep coming here to draw water." . . .

- Jesus begins with his own physical thirst and ends up talking about the woman's soul thirst. What can I learn from this conversation about sharing the good news?

- In speaking with a woman to whom he was not related, and to a Samaritan, who was considered apostate by the Jewish community, Jesus crossed two cultural boundaries. What boundaries do I face in a normal day?

Monday 20th March
Saint Joseph, Spouse of the Blessed Virgin Mary
Matthew 1:16, 18–21, 24a

Jacob [was] the father of Joseph the husband of Mary, of whom Jesus was born, who is called the Messiah. . . . Now the birth of Jesus the Messiah took place in this way. When his mother Mary had been engaged to Joseph, but before they lived together, she was found to be with child from the Holy Spirit. Her husband Joseph, being a righteous man and unwilling to expose her to public disgrace, planned to dismiss her quietly. But just when he had resolved to do this, an angel of the Lord appeared to him in a dream and said, "Joseph, son of David, do not be afraid to take Mary as your wife, for the child conceived in her is from the Holy Spirit. She will bear a son, and you are to name him Jesus, for he will save his people from their sins." . . . When Joseph awoke from sleep, he did as the angel of the Lord commanded him; he took her as his wife . . .

- A great quality of Joseph was his openness to God. Something happened in a dream that led him to trust in the call of God even in the strange circumstances of the pregnancy of his wife-to-be. Lord, help me open my thoughts, dreams, and desires to your influence.

- Saint Matthew tells the story of Jesus from Joseph's viewpoint. He is shown as an ordinary, good Jew, obedient to the Law. God intervenes and shatters his expectations. He is called to a new level of obedience. Lord, am I open to letting you break in on my life?

Tuesday 21st March
Matthew 18:21–35

Then Peter came and said to him, "Lord, if another member of the church sins against me, how often should I forgive? As many as seven times?" Jesus said to him, "Not seven times, but, I tell you, seventy-seven times. For this reason the kingdom of heaven may be compared to a king who wished to settle accounts with his slaves. When he began the reckoning, one who owed him ten thousand talents was brought to him; and, as he could not pay, his lord ordered him to be sold, together with his wife and children and all his possessions, and payment to be made. So the slave fell on his knees before him, saying, 'Have patience with me, and I will pay you everything.' And out of pity for him, the lord of that slave released him and forgave him the debt. But that same slave, as he went out, came upon one of his fellow slaves who owed him a hundred denarii; and seizing him by the throat, he said, 'Pay what you owe.' Then his fellow slave fell down and pleaded with him, 'Have patience with me, and I will pay you.' But he refused; then he went and threw him into prison until he would pay the debt. When his fellow slaves saw what had happened, they were greatly distressed, and they went and reported to their lord all that had taken place. Then his lord summoned him and said to him, 'You wicked slave! I forgave you all that debt because you pleaded with me. Should you not have had mercy on your fellow slave, as I had mercy on you?' And in anger his lord handed him over to be tortured until he would pay his entire debt. So my heavenly Father will also do to every one of you, if you do not forgive your brother or sister from your heart."

- Only those who forgive belong in God's kingdom. Lord, to forgive from the heart is a grace I must pray for. I can't do it on my own, and I know this.

I can be so hard-hearted with those who offend me. Have mercy on me and change my heart!

- When God is at work, there is no purely private benefit; the effects spread widely. As I acknowledge that what is good in my life comes from God, I pray for the generosity I need to be a blessing to others.

Wednesday 22nd March
Matthew 5:17–19

Jesus said to the crowds, "Do not think that I have come to abolish the law or the prophets; I have come not to abolish but to fulfill. For truly I tell you, until heaven and earth pass away, not one letter, not one stroke of a letter, will pass from the law until all is accomplished. Therefore, whoever breaks one of the least of these commandments, and teaches others to do the same, will be called least in the kingdom of heaven; but whoever does them and teaches them will be called great in the kingdom of heaven."

- Lord, you were not turning your back on the past but deepening our sense of where we stand before God: not as scrupulous rule keepers but as loving children.

- Christians continue to reverence the Old Testament as a source of revelation—for instance, by praying the psalms. Do I appreciate how such prayer brings me into harmony with my Jewish brothers and sisters today?

Thursday 23rd March
Luke 11:14–23

Now Jesus was casting out a demon that was mute; when the demon had gone out, the one who had been mute spoke, and the crowds were amazed. But some of them said, "He casts out demons by Beelzebul, the ruler of the demons." Others, to test him, kept demanding from him a sign from heaven. But he knew what they were thinking and said to them, "Every kingdom divided against itself becomes a desert, and house falls on house. If Satan also is divided against himself, how will his kingdom stand?—for you say that I cast out the demons by Beelzebul. Now if I cast out the demons by Beelzebul, by whom do your exorcists cast them out? Therefore they will be your judges. But if it is by the finger of God that I cast out the demons, then the kingdom of God has come to you. When a strong man, fully armed, guards his castle, his property is safe. But when one stronger than he attacks him and overpowers him, he takes away his armour in which he trusted and divides his plunder. Whoever is not with me is against me, and whoever does not gather with me scatters."

- With whom do I identify in the crowd that witnesses Jesus' miracle? With those who watch in amazed belief? With those who reject him? Or with those who hedge their bets, looking for further signs? Jesus forces us off the middle ground. Today, Jesus, do I believe in your power in my life?

- Jesus' mission is to overcome evil in all its forms. I thank God for this. *Satan* means "adversary" and refers to all that stands against the goodness of God. I may live under a corrupt government, where bad legislation oppresses the innocent and unfair taxes enrich the powerful. I may be called by God to protest against wrongdoing. I can also pray!

Friday 24th March
Mark 12:28–34

One of the scribes came near and heard them disputing with one another, and seeing that Jesus answered them well, he asked him, "Which commandment is the first of all?" Jesus answered, "The first is, 'Hear, O Israel: the Lord our God, the Lord is one; you shall love the Lord your God with all your heart, and with all your soul, and with all your mind, and with all your strength.' The second is this, 'You shall love your neighbor as yourself.' There is no other commandment greater than these." Then the scribe said to him, "You are right, Teacher; you have truly said that 'he is one, and besides him there is no other'; and 'to love him with all the heart, and with all the understanding, and with all the strength,' and 'to love one's neighbor as oneself,'—this is much more important than all whole burnt offerings and sacrifices." When Jesus saw that he answered wisely, he said to him, "You are not far from the kingdom of God." After that no one dared to ask him any question.

- Are you comfortable with the designation of love as a *commandment*? That word can sound cold and legalistic, whereas the word *love* evokes warmth and freedom. Could you suggest an alternative to commandment? Or would you want to?

- Lord, with what affection and regard you answered this scribe. Unlike others, he was seeking wisdom, not an argument. He relished Jesus' answer and placed it in the context of the Scriptures. Is my search as serious as that scribe's?

Saturday 25th March
The Annunciation of the Lord
Luke 1:26–38

In the sixth month the angel Gabriel was sent by God to a town in Galilee called Nazareth, to a virgin engaged to a man whose name was Joseph, of the house of David. The virgin's name was Mary. And he came to her and said, "Greetings, favored one! The Lord is with you." But she was much perplexed by his words and pondered what sort of greeting this might be. The angel said to her, "Do not be afraid, Mary, for you have found favor with God. And now, you will conceive in your womb and bear a son, and you will name him Jesus. He will be great, and will be called the Son of the Most High, and the Lord God will give to him the throne of his ancestor David. He will reign over the house of Jacob forever, and of his king-dom there will be no end." Mary said to the angel, "How can this be, since I am a virgin?" The angel said to her, "The Holy Spirit will come upon you, and the power of the Most High will overshadow you; therefore the child to be born will be holy; he will be called Son of God. And now, your relative Elizabeth in her old age has also conceived a son; and this is the sixth month for her who was said to be barren. For nothing will be impossible with God." Then Mary said, "Here am I, the servant of the Lord; let it be with me according to your word." Then the angel de-parted from her.

- Mary is not flattered but perplexed, and she voic-es her perplexity. She hears God's messenger but wonders, *Can this be true?* She knows that she is free to say yes or no. She ponders the invitation in her heart, then gives her response. Seat of Wisdom, teach me how to use my head and heart in a crisis.

- "Let it be with me according to your word." Lord, this is not an easy prayer to make. You prayed it yourself in Gethsemane in a sweat of blood: not my will but yours be done. Help me make it the pattern of my life.

The Fourth Week of Lent
March 26—April 1

Something to think and pray about each day this week:

Jesus' Humanity

In contemplating the Gospels during Lent, take this advice to heart: Be sure to take Jesus' humanity seriously even as you reflect on his divine attributes. God took humanity seriously enough to become one of us, and we do God a disservice if we downplay what God has done in becoming human. When we use our imagination in contemplating Jesus, we trust that God's Spirit will use it to reveal something about Jesus that is important for us so that we will love him and want to follow him. The only way we can get to know another person is through revelation; the other must reveal him- or herself to us. In contemplating the Gospels, we are asking Jesus to reveal himself to us.

—William A. Barry, SJ, *Lenten Meditations*

The Presence of God

"I stand at the door and knock," says the Lord. What a wonderful privilege that the Lord of all creation desires to come to me. I welcome his presence.

Freedom

Saint Ignatius thought that a thick and shapeless tree trunk would never believe that it could become a statue, admired as a miracle of sculpture, and would never submit itself to the chisel of the sculptor, who sees by her genius what she can make of it.

I ask for the grace to let myself be shaped by my loving Creator.

Consciousness

Knowing that God loves me unconditionally, I can afford to be honest about how I am. What are my fears and desires? What do I expect from God? What am I willing to give to God—from my emotions and talents, thoughts and energy? And how do I feel now? I share my feelings openly with the Lord.

The Word
I take my time to read the Word of God, slowly, a few times, allowing myself to dwell on anything that strikes me. (Please turn to the Scripture on the following pages. Inspiration points are there should you need them. When you are ready, return here to continue.)

Conversation
Do I notice myself reacting as I pray with the Word of God? Do I feel challenged, comforted, angry? Imagining Jesus sitting or standing by me, I speak out my feelings, as one trusted friend to another.

Conclusion
I thank God for these moments we have spent together and for any insights I have been given concerning the text.

Sunday 26th March
Fourth Sunday of Lent

John 9:1, 6–9, 13–17, 34–38

As he walked along, he saw a man blind from birth. . . . When he had said this, he spat on the ground and made mud with the saliva and spread the mud on the man's eyes, saying to him, "Go, wash in the pool of Siloam" (which means Sent). Then he went and washed and came back able to see. The neighbors and those who had seen him before as a beggar began to ask, "Is this not the man who used to sit and beg?" Some were saying, "It is he." Others were saying, "No, but it is someone like him." He kept saying, "I am the man." . . . They brought to the Pharisees the man who had formerly been blind. Now it was a sabbath day when Jesus made the mud and opened his eyes. Then the Pharisees also began to ask him how he had received his sight. He said to them, "He put mud on my eyes. Then I washed, and now I see." Some of the Pharisees said, "This man is not from God, for he does not observe the sabbath." But others said, "How can a man who is a sinner perform such signs?" And they were divided. So they said again to the blind man, "What do you say about him? It was your eyes he opened." He said, "He is a prophet." . . . They answered him, "You were born entirely in sins, and are you trying to teach us?" And they drove him out. Jesus heard that they had driven him out, and when he found him, he said, "Do you believe in the Son of Man?" He answered, "And who is he, sir? Tell me, so that I may believe in him." Jesus said to him, "You have seen him, and the one speaking with you is he." He said, "Lord, I believe." And he worshipped him.

- The opening question of the disciples was, "Who is to blame?" This is a common question in the media today; perhaps it is part of my own vocabulary. Jesus reminds us that sometimes no one is to blame but that difficult situations present an opportunity for us to be drawn into God's presence.

- Lord, there were times I was lost and found, was blind and then could see. Thank you. The man's blindness is cured, but the blindness of those who won't believe in Jesus remains. I think of how I grope, stumble, and am unsure of my direction unless I can rely on Jesus, the light of the world.

Monday 27th March
John 4:43–54

When the two days were over, he went from that place to Galilee (for Jesus himself had testified that a prophet has no honor in the prophet's own country). When he came to Galilee, the Galileans welcomed him, since they had seen all that he had done in Jerusalem at the festival; for they too had gone to the festival. Then he came again to Cana in Galilee where he had changed the water into wine. Now there was a royal official whose son lay ill in Capernaum. When he heard that Jesus had come from Judea to Galilee, he went and begged him to come down and heal his son, for he was at the point of death. Then Jesus said to him, "Unless you see signs and wonders you will not believe." The official said to him, "Sir, come down before my little boy dies." Jesus said to him, "Go; your son will live." The man believed the word that Jesus spoke to him and started on his way. As he was going down, his slaves met him and told him that his child was alive. So he asked them the hour when he began to recover, and they said to him, "Yesterday at one in the afternoon the fever left him." The father realized that this was the hour when Jesus had said to him, "Your son will live." So he himself believed, along with his whole household. Now this was the second sign that Jesus did after coming from Judea to Galilee.

- This prayer was made humbly and wholeheartedly, and by a Gentile. Jesus saw true faith in this man's prayer; the boy was healed through the faith of his father. May I readily bring people of all sorts to Jesus for healing.

- This is the first recorded healing miracle of Jesus. Do I believe in miracles? More important, do I believe that Jesus is the greatest miracle of the universe? He is all the love of God contained in a human heart and a human face (Pope Benedict XVI).

Tuesday 28th March
John 5:1–16

There was a festival of the Jews, and Jesus went up to Jerusalem. Now in Jerusalem by the Sheep Gate there is a pool, called in Hebrew Beth-zatha, which has five porticoes. In these lay many invalids—blind, lame, and paralyzed. One man was there who had been ill for thirty-eight years. When Jesus saw him lying there and knew that he had been there a long time, he said to him, "Do you want to be made well?" The sick man answered him, "Sir, I have no one to put me into the pool when the water is stirred up; and while I am making my way, someone else steps down ahead of me." Jesus said to him, "Stand up, take your mat and walk." At once the man was made well, and he took up his mat and began to walk. Now that day was a sabbath. So the Jews said to the man who had been cured, "It is the sabbath; it is not lawful for you to carry your mat." But he answered them, "The man who made me well said to me, Take up your mat and walk." They asked him, "Who is the man who said to you, Take it up and walk?" Now the man who had been healed did not know who it was, for Jesus had disappeared in the crowd that was there. Later Jesus found him in the temple and said to him, "See, you have been made well! Do not sin any more, so that nothing worse happens to you." The man went away and told the Jews that it was Jesus who had made him well. Therefore the Jews started persecuting Jesus, because he was doing such things on the sabbath.

- The man on the mat is obviously ill, and yet Jesus asks if he wants to be made well. In truth, sometimes we prefer to remain as we are rather than change for the better. We fear what the change will bring, or we have grown comfortable with our "illness." I imagine Jesus asking me, right now, "Do you want to be made well?" What is my response?

- By healing people on the Sabbath, Jesus was breaking not the law of Moses but subsequent laws created to help people know how to fulfill the law of Moses. It can seem simpler to stick with rigid and complicated systems than to rely on our own discernment of what God asks of us. What discernment is required of me today?

Wednesday 29th March

John 5:17–30

Jesus answered them, "My Father is still working, and I also am working." For this reason the Jews were seeking all the more to kill him, because he was not only breaking the sabbath, but was also calling God his own Father, thereby making himself equal to God. Jesus said to them, "Very truly, I tell you, the Son can do nothing on his own, but only what he sees the Father doing; for whatever the Father does, the Son does likewise. The Father loves the Son and shows him all that he himself is doing; and he will show him greater works than these, so that you will be astonished. Indeed, just as the Father raises the dead and gives them life, so also the Son gives life to whomsoever he wishes. The Father judges no one but has given all judgment to the Son, so that all may honor the Son just as they honor the Father. Anyone who does not honor the Son does not honor the Father who sent him. Very truly, I tell you, anyone who hears my word and believes him who sent me has eternal life, and does not come under judgment, but has passed from death to life. Very truly, I tell you, the hour is coming, and is now here, when the dead will hear the voice of the Son of God, and those who hear will live. For just as the Father has life in himself, so he has granted the Son also to have life in himself; and he has given him authority to execute judgment, because he is the Son of Man. Do not be astonished at this; for the hour is coming when all who are in their graves will hear his voice and will come out—those who have done good, to the resurrection of life, and those who have done evil, to the resurrection of condemnation. I can do nothing on my own. As I hear, I judge; and my judgment is just, because I seek to do not my own will but the will of him who sent me."

- Note the striking statement: "My Father is still working, and I also am working." God is present among us, but this is not a passive presence. It is an active presence through which God is involved in the drama of our lives.

- It is hard to understand the relationships between divinity and humanity, but we can enter prayer with the willingness and hope to fulfill the will of God. Our time in prayer, silent or verbal, is our wish that God's will be done and that the love of his reign be made visible on earth.

Thursday 30th March
John 5:31–47

Jesus said, "If I testify about myself, my testimony is not true. There is another who testifies on my behalf, and I know that his testimony to me is true. You sent messengers to John, and he testified to the truth. Not that I accept such human testimony, but I say these things so that you may be saved. He was a burning and shining lamp, and you were willing to rejoice for a while in his light. But I have a testimony greater than John's. . . ."

- Jesus appeals to the minds of those who seek to disregard him. He reminds them of what they have seen, of the witnesses they have heard, and of the words of the prophets. I pray that I be blessed with deeper faith as I review the evidence to which Jesus draws my attention. As I believe in Jesus who was sent by God, the Word of God is alive in me.

- John the Baptist prepared the way for people to hear Jesus. He brought people near to God, and some of them recognized Jesus when he arrived. Some people we meet make it easier to recognize Jesus. It is good to have met people who are like Jesus—just as John the Baptist prepared the way of Jesus by the way he lived. Give thanks for such people in prayer!

Friday 31st March
John 7:1–2, 10, 25–30

Jesus went about in Galilee. He did not wish to go about in Judea because the Jews were looking for an opportunity to kill him. Now the Jewish festival of

Booths was near. . . . But after his brothers had gone to the festival, then he also went, not publicly but as it were in secret. . . . Now some of the people of Jerusalem were saying, "Is not this the man whom they are trying to kill? And here he is, speaking openly, but they say nothing to him! Can it be that the authorities really know that this is the Messiah? Yet we know where this man is from; but when the Messiah comes, no one will know where he is from." Then Jesus cried out as he was teaching in the temple, "You know me, and you know where I am from. I have not come on my own. But the one who sent me is true, and you do not know him. I know him, because I am from him, and he sent me." Then they tried to arrest him, but no one laid hands on him, because his hour had not yet come.

- Jesus knew throughout his passion where he came from—the heart of God the Father. He knew he would return there. He always knew he was not on his own. Can we walk with him in his passion of today? Where people suffer, Jesus suffers.

- The arguments go to and fro about Jesus: Some say that they know nothing about him, others that they know everything. It seems that nowadays, too, there are experts on every side. I realize that Lent calls me, not to be convinced in my mind but to accept Jesus in my heart. Show me how to learn of you in that way, Jesus.

Saturday 1st April

John 7:40–53

When they heard Jesus' words, some in the crowd said, "This is really the prophet." Others said, "This is the Messiah." But some asked, "Surely the Messiah does not come from Galilee, does he? Has not the Scripture said that the Messiah is descended from David and comes from Bethlehem, the village where David lived?" So there was a division in the crowd because of him. Some of them wanted to arrest him, but no one laid hands on him. Then the temple police went back to the chief priests and Pharisees, who asked them, "Why did you not arrest him?" The police answered, "Never has anyone spoken like this!" Then the Pharisees replied, "Surely you have not been deceived too, have you? Has any one of the authorities or of the Pharisees believed in him? But this crowd, which does not know the law—they are accursed." Nicodemus, who had gone to Jesus before, and who was one of them, asked, "Our law does not judge people without first giving them a hearing to find out what they are doing, does it?" They replied, "Surely you are not also from Galilee, are you? Search and you will see that no prophet is to arise from Galilee." Then each of them went home.

• Prayer can allow us to be surprised by Jesus Christ—or to be questioned by him. We can end our prayer with the question, "Who is this man, and what have I learned about him today?" He gives no easy answers but walks with us while we ask the questions.

• The police were sent to Jesus to arrest him, but they came back empty-handed, exclaiming, "Never has anyone spoken like this!" Familiarity can blunt us to the revolutionary power of Christ's words. Lord, grant that I may hear and understand and be turned inside out.

The Fifth Week of Lent
April 2—April 8

Something to think and pray about each day this week:

The Eternal Broken Heart

In Jesus, God saves us by becoming so vulnerable that we are able to kill him in a vile and humiliating way. The crucifixion and resurrection of Jesus assure us that God's offer of friendship will never be withdrawn, no matter what we do. If the cross did not result in a withdrawal of the offer, then nothing we do will lead to a change of God's heart. We can, however, refuse the offer. Friendship is a mutual relationship, and a person has to accept the offer; he or she cannot be coerced or tricked into it. And any human being's final refusal of God's friendship breaks God's heart. Still, God does not turn away from such a person in anger and rage. God lives eternally with a broken heart. That's how vulnerable God wants to be.

—William A. Barry, SJ, *Lenten Meditations*

The Presence of God

To be present is to arrive as one is and open up to the other.

At this instant, as I arrive here, God is present waiting for me.

God always arrives before me, desiring to connect with me

even more than my most intimate friend.

I take a moment and greet my loving God.

Freedom

I am free. When I look at these words in writing, they seem to create in me a feeling of awe. Yes, a wonderful feeling of freedom. Thank you, God.

Consciousness

To be conscious about something is to be aware of it. Dear Lord, help me remember that you gave me life. Thank you for the gift of life.

Teach me to slow down, to be still and enjoy the pleasures created for me. To be aware of the beauty that surrounds me. The marvel of mountains, the calmness of lakes, the fragility of a flower petal. I need to remember that all these things come from you.

The Word
The Word of God comes to us through the Scriptures.
May the Holy Spirit enlighten my mind and heart to
respond to the Gospel teachings. (Please turn to the
Scripture on the following pages. Inspiration points
are there should you need them. When you are ready,
return here to continue.)

Conversation
I begin to talk to Jesus about the Scripture I have just
read. What part of it strikes a chord in me? Perhaps
the words of a friend—or some story I heard recently—will slowly rise to the surface in my consciousness. If so, does the story throw light on what the
Scripture passage may be trying to say to me?

Conclusion
Glory be to the Father, and to the Son, and to the
Holy Spirit,
As it was in the beginning, is now and ever shall be,
World without end. Amen.

Sunday 2nd April
Fifth Sunday of Lent
John 11:3–7, 17, 20–27, 33b–45

So the sisters sent a message to Jesus, "Lord, he whom you love is ill." But when Jesus heard it, he said, "This illness does not lead to death; rather it is for God's glory, so that the Son of God may be glorified through it." Accordingly, though Jesus loved Martha and her sister and Lazarus, after having heard that Lazarus was ill, he stayed two days longer in the place where he was. Then after this he said to the disciples, "Let us go to Judea again." . . . When Jesus arrived, he found that Lazarus had already been in the tomb for four days. . . . When Martha heard that Jesus was coming, she went and met him, while Mary stayed at home. Martha said to Jesus, "Lord, if you had been here, my brother would not have died. But even now I know that God will give you whatever you ask of him." Jesus said to her, "Your brother will rise again." Martha said to him, "I know that he will rise again in the resurrection on the last day." Jesus said to her, "I am the resurrection and the life. Those who believe in me, even though they die, will live, and everyone who lives and believes in me will never die. Do you believe this?" She said to him, "Yes, Lord, I believe that you are the Messiah, the Son of God, the one coming into the world." . . . When Jesus saw her weeping, and the Jews who came with her also weeping, he was greatly disturbed in spirit and deeply moved. He said, "Where have you laid him?" They said to him, "Lord, come and see." Jesus began to weep. So the Jews said, "See how he loved him!" But some of them said, "Could not he who opened the eyes of the blind man have kept this man from dying?" Then Jesus, again greatly disturbed, came to the tomb. It was a cave, and a stone was lying against it. Jesus said, "Take away the stone." Martha, the sister of the dead man, said to him, "Lord, already there is a stench because he has been dead for four days." Jesus said to her, "Did I not tell you that if you believed, you would see the glory of God?" So they took away the stone. And Jesus looked upwards and said, "Father, I thank you for having heard me. I knew that you always hear me, but I have said this for the sake of the crowd standing here, so that they may believe that you sent me." When he had said this, he cried with a loud voice, "Lazarus, come out!" The dead man came out, his hands and feet bound with strips of cloth, and his face wrapped in a cloth. Jesus said to them, "Unbind him, and let him go." Many of the Jews therefore, who had come with Mary and had seen what Jesus did, believed in him.

• I hear you asking me the same question, Lord: "Do you believe that I am the resurrection and the life?" In the long run, nothing is more important than my answer to this. I cannot grasp your words in my imagination, Lord, but I believe. Help my unbelief.

- "Unbind him, and let him go." Even a man resurrected from the dead needed the help of community. Show me, Lord, how I can participate in others' unbinding and freedom.

Monday 3rd April
John 8:1–11

Early in the morning Jesus came again to the temple. All the people came to him and he sat down and began to teach them. The scribes and the Pharisees brought a woman who had been caught in adultery; and making her stand before all of them, they said to him, "Teacher, this woman was caught in the very act of committing adultery. Now in the law Moses commanded us to stone such women. Now what do you say?" They said this to test him, so that they might have some charge to bring against him. Jesus bent down and wrote with his finger on the ground. When they kept on questioning him, he straightened up and said to them, "Let anyone among you who is without sin be the first to throw a stone at her." And once again he bent down and wrote on the ground. When they heard it, they went away, one by one, beginning with the elders; and Jesus was left alone with the woman standing before him. Jesus straightened up and said to her, "Woman, where are they? Has no one condemned you?" She said, "No one, sir." And Jesus said, "Neither do I condemn you. Go your way, and from now on do not sin again."

- With whom do you most identify in this story? The adulterous woman who, though guilty, did not deserve death by stoning? (Besides, where was her partner in adultery? Was he not equally guilty?) Or do you see yourself in those who condemned her, shamed her publicly, and were willing to stone her?

- As I reflect on my life and consider my need for forgiveness, I realize that I need to draw closer to Jesus, who loves me. I hear Jesus speaking to me— not condemning me, but giving me a new mission and a new vision of myself.

Tuesday 4th April
John 8:21–30

Jesus said to them, "I am going away, and you will search for me, but you will die in your sin. Where I am going, you cannot come." Then the Jews said, "Is he going to kill himself? Is that what he means by saying, Where I am going, you cannot come?" He said to them, "You are from below, I am from above; you are of this world, I am not of this world. I told you that you would die in your sins, for you will die in your sins unless you believe that I am he." They said to him, "Who are you?" Jesus said to them, "Why do I speak to you at all? I have much to say about you and much to condemn; but the one who sent me is true, and I declare to the world what I have heard from him." They did not understand that he was speaking to them about the Father. So Jesus said, "When you have lifted up the Son of Man, then you will realize that I am he, and that I do nothing on my own, but I speak these things as the Father instructed me. And the one who sent me is with me; he has not left me alone, for I always do what is pleasing to him." As he was saying these things, many believed in him.

- The readings of these days may need to be simplified when brought to prayer. You might take a single verse, or even a single phrase. For example, "The one who sent me is with me; he has not left me alone." Or sit quietly with the overall mystery of who Jesus is.

- When I knock on God's door, Jesus opens it and invites me in to meet his Father! "I always do what is pleasing to the Father." This reveals the heart of Jesus' spirituality. I pray that it may become the truth of my life, too, because God is so good to me.

Wednesday 5th April

John 8:31–42

Then Jesus said to the Jews who had believed in him, "If you continue in my word, you are truly my disciples; and you will know the truth, and the truth will make you free." They answered him, "We are descendants of Abraham and have never been slaves to anyone. What do you mean by saying, 'You will be made free'?" Jesus answered them, "Very truly, I tell you, everyone who commits sin is a slave to sin. The slave does not have a permanent place in the household; the son has a place there forever. So if the Son makes you free, you will be free indeed. I know that you are descendants of Abraham; yet you look for an opportunity to kill me, because there is no place in you for my word. I declare what I have seen in the Father's presence; as for you, you should do what you have heard from the Father." They answered him, "Abraham is our father." Jesus said to them, "If you were Abraham's children, you would be doing what Abraham did, but now you are trying to kill me, a man who has told you the truth that I heard from God. This is not what Abraham did. You are indeed doing what your father does." They said to him, "We are not illegitimate children; we have one father, God himself." Jesus said to them, "If God were your Father, you would love me, for I came from

God and now I am here. I did not come on my own, but he sent me."

- *Abiding* ("continue in") means that we draw life from the Word of God. This life is Christ himself; he is the love of the Father. Being a disciple, a listener, is living and abiding in truth, knowing that the Jesus of our prayer comes from God and is with God.

- Our love indicates our spiritual pedigree. Jesus, help me follow you and thus accept truth and demonstrate it through love.

Thursday 6th April
John 8:51–59

Jesus said, "Very truly, I tell you, whoever keeps my word will never see death." The Jews said to him, "Now we know that you have a demon. Abraham died, and so did the prophets; yet you say, Whoever keeps my word will never taste death. Are you greater than our father Abraham, who died? The prophets also died. Who do you claim to be?" Jesus answered, "If I glorify myself, my glory is nothing. It is my Father who glorifies me, he of whom you say, He is our God, though you do not know him. But I know him; if I were to say that I do not know him, I would be a liar like you. But I do know him and I keep his word. Your ancestor Abraham rejoiced that he would see my day; he saw it and was glad." Then the Jews said to him, "You are not yet fifty years old, and have you seen Abraham?" Jesus said to them, "Very truly, I tell you, before Abraham was, I am." So they picked up stones to throw at him, but Jesus hid himself and went out of the temple.

- Note yet another "I am" statement: *Before Abraham was, I am.* Jesus claims both preexistence and one-ness with God. How does such information influ-ence the way I think about life and death and what it means to be a spiritual being?

- Jesus is saying, "If you want to see God, here I am!" What should be a wonderful moment of revelation becomes horribly negative. Execution by stoning was the punishment for asserting that one is equal to God. Lord, I find you in some safe place and try to comfort you. What more can you do to show people who you are?

Friday 7th April
John 10:31–42

The Jews took up stones again to stone him. Jesus replied, "I have shown you many good works from the Father. For which of these are you going to stone me?" The Jews answered, "It is not for a good work that we are going to stone you, but for blasphemy, be-cause you, though only a human being, are making yourself God." Jesus answered, "Is it not written in your law, 'I said, you are gods'? If those to whom the Word of God came were called 'gods'—and the Scripture cannot be annulled—can you say that the one whom the Father has sanctified and sent into the world is blaspheming because I said, 'I am God's Son'? If I am not doing the works of my Father, then do not believe me. But if I do them, even though you do not believe me, believe the works, so that you may know and understand that the Father is in me and I am in the Father." Then they tried to arrest him again, but he escaped from their hands. He went away again across the Jordan to the place where John had been baptizing earlier, and he remained there. Many came to him, and they were saying, John performed no sign, but everything that John said about this man was true. And many believed in him there.

- Jesus often impresses upon us the need to act. One can argue with words, but deeds speak for themselves. The word is planted deep in me, and I pray according to the words of the apostle James, "Let me be a doer of the word and not a forgetful hearer."

- The world watches the deeds of Christians and is often not impressed. The people in today's reading condemn Jesus because of their particular image of God. What is my image of God? Have I ever condemned someone because I nursed a warped image of God?

Saturday 8th April
John 11:45–56

Many of the Jews therefore, who had come with Mary and had seen what Jesus did, believed in him. But some of them went to the Pharisees and told them what he had done. So the chief priests and the Pharisees called a meeting of the council, and said, "What are we to do? This man is performing many signs. If we let him go on like this, everyone will believe in him, and the Romans will come and destroy both our holy place and our nation." But one of them, Caiaphas, who was high priest that year, said to them, "You know nothing at all! You do not understand that it is better for you to have one man die for the people than to have the whole nation destroyed." He did not say this on his own, but being high priest that year he prophesied that Jesus was about to die for the nation, and not for the nation only, but to gather into one the dispersed children of God. So from that day on they planned to put him to death. Jesus therefore no longer walked about openly among the Jews, but went from there to a town called Ephraim in the region near the wilderness; and he remained there with the disciples. Now the Passover of the Jews was near, and many went up from the country to Jerusalem before the Passover to purify themselves. They were looking for Jesus and were asking one another as they stood in the temple, "What do you think? Surely he will not come to the festival, will he?"

- Caiaphas is ruthless, political, and determined to buttress the status quo and the privileges of his wealthy class. He uses the argument of the powerful in every age: we must eliminate the awkward troublemaker in the name of the common good. But he says more than he knows. One man, Jesus, will die for the people—and for all of us.

- Caiaphas is afraid that the popularity of Jesus will draw down the wrath of Rome and destroy both the temple—the holy place—and the nation. In his blindness he cannot see that the Jewish people are themselves the temple. Do I appreciate that I, too, am a temple of the living God? Lord, take away my blindness so that I can see myself as you see me.

Holy Week
April 9—April 15

Something to think and pray about each day this week:

Facing Evil

Jesus lived a human life as God's true Son, overcoming the temptations all of us inherit by being born into this world. On Good Friday, Jesus went to his death trusting that his dear Father would bring victory out of what seemed the total defeat of his mission. In the garden on the night before his death, he seems to have faced for the last time the temptation to fear, but he was able to hand over his life in trust to his Father. He went to his death believing that his way of being Messiah was the way to bring about God's Kingdom, and he absorbed human evil without passing it on. His faith made this possible. *Jesus, help me face the evil of the world with the faith you demonstrated on Good Friday.*

—William A. Barry, SJ, *Lenten Meditations*

The Presence of God
Be still and know that I am God. Lord, may your Spirit guide me to seek your loving presence more and more. For it is there I find rest and refreshment from this busy world.

Freedom
By God's grace I was born to live in freedom. Free to enjoy the pleasures he created for me. Dear Lord, grant that I may live as you intended, with complete confidence in your loving care.

Consciousness
In God's loving presence I unwind the past day, starting from now and looking back, moment by moment.
I gather in all the goodness and light, in gratitude.
I attend to the shadows and what they say to me, seeking healing, courage, forgiveness.

The Word
The Word of God comes to us through the Scriptures. May the Holy Spirit enlighten my mind and heart to respond to the Gospel teachings. (Please turn to the Scripture on the following pages. Inspiration points are there should you need them. When you are ready, return here to continue.)

Conversation

Jesus, you always welcomed little children when you walked on this earth. Teach me to have a childlike trust in you, to live in the knowledge that you will never abandon me.

Conclusion

Glory be to the Father, and to the Son, and to the Holy Spirit,
As it was in the beginning, is now and ever shall be,
World without end. Amen.

Sunday 9th April
Palm Sunday of the Passion of the Lord
Matthew 26:14—27:66

Then one of the twelve, who was called Judas Iscariot, went to the chief priests and said, "What will you give me if I betray him to you?" They paid him thirty pieces of silver. And from that moment he began to look for an opportunity to betray him. On the first day of Unleavened Bread the disciples came to Jesus, saying, "Where do you want us to make the preparations for you to eat the Passover?" He said, "Go into the city to a certain man, and say to him, 'The Teacher says, My time is near; I will keep the Passover at your house with my disciples.'" So the disciples did as Jesus had directed them, and they prepared the Passover meal. When it was evening, he took his place with the twelve; and while they were eating, he said, "Truly I tell you, one of you will betray me." And they became greatly distressed and began to say to him one after another, "Surely not I, Lord?" He answered, "The one who has dipped his hand into the bowl with me will betray me. The Son of Man goes as it is written of him, but woe to that one by whom the Son of Man is betrayed! It would have been better for that one not to have been born." Judas, who betrayed him, said, "Surely not I, Rabbi?" He replied, "You have said so.". . .

- Look at Judas and watch him—fearfully betraying Jesus. Look at Jesus as his heart goes out to the weakness of his disciples. In all sorts of weakness in our lives, the love of God is triumphant. Let him be the strength in your weakness and sinfulness.

- Is Judas motivated by anger and disappointment? Had he a different vision of the messianic kingdom than Jesus? Did he resent that Jesus saw through him when he protested at the waste of Mary's costly ointment at the feast? One thing is clear: he refused to accept Jesus as he was. Like us, he didn't see that it is we, not God, who must change.

Monday 10th April

John 12:1–11

Six days before the Passover Jesus came to Bethany, the home of Lazarus, whom he had raised from the dead. There they gave a dinner for him. Martha served, and Lazarus was one of those at the table with him. Mary took a pound of costly perfume made of pure nard, anointed Jesus' feet, and wiped them with her hair. The house was filled with the fragrance of the perfume. But Judas Iscariot, one of his disciples (the one who was about to betray him), said, "Why was this perfume not sold for three hundred denarii and the money given to the poor?" (He said this not because he cared about the poor, but because he was a thief; he kept the common purse and used to steal what was put into it.) Jesus said, "Leave her alone. She bought it so that she might keep it for the day of my burial. You always have the poor with you, but you do not always have me." When the great crowd of the Jews learned that he was there, they came not only because of Jesus but also to see Lazarus, whom he had raised from the dead. So the chief priests planned to put Lazarus to death as well, since it was on account of him that many of the Jews were deserting and were believing in Jesus.

- We join the dinner party and are struck by the surpassing generosity of Mary's gesture, and then by the bitter begrudging with which Judas interprets the gift. We might allow moments of prayer this week to reach the zones within us that need tolerance, healing, and forgiveness.

- The generosity of Mary appeared wasteful and misplaced. Mary knew that Jesus was worthy of her honor and service, even when it cost. She was not held back by the judgments of others. Jesus, may I give to you freely and not care about others' opinions and reactions.

Tuesday 11th April

John 13:21–33, 36–38

Jesus was troubled in spirit, and declared, "Very truly, I tell you, one of you will betray me." The disciples looked at one another, uncertain of whom he was speaking. One of his disciples—the one whom Jesus loved—was reclining next to him; Simon Peter therefore motioned to him to ask Jesus of whom he was speaking. So while reclining next to Jesus, he asked him, "Lord, who is it?" Jesus answered, "It is the one to whom I give this piece of bread when I have dipped it in the dish." So when he had dipped the piece of bread, he gave it to Judas son of Simon Iscariot. After he received the piece of bread, Satan entered into him. Jesus said to him, "Do quickly what you are going to do." Now no one at the table knew why he said this to him. Some thought that, because Judas had the common purse, Jesus was telling him, "Buy what we need for the festival"; or, that he should give something to the poor. So, after receiving the piece of bread, he immediately went out. And it was night. When he had gone out, Jesus said, "Now the Son of Man has been glorified, and God has been glorified in him. If God has been glorified in him, God will also glorify him in himself and will glorify him at once. . . . Simon Peter said to him, "Lord, where are you going?" Jesus answered, "Where I am going, you cannot follow me now; but you will follow afterwards." Peter said to him, "Lord, why can I not follow you now? I will lay down my life for you." Jesus answered, "Will you lay down your life for me? Very truly, I tell you, before the cock crows, you will have denied me three times."

- Imagine yourself at the table during the Last Supper. Are you picking up the tensions among the other participants? Do you notice how Jesus is troubled in spirit? Let the drama of the scene draw you into it. What are your predominant feelings? Speak freely to Jesus about the whole situation and your reactions to it.

- Two treacheries: Judas went out to grab his money, betray Jesus, and kill himself in despair. Peter denied his Lord, faced his own appalling guilt, and wept bitterly—but failure was not the end of his mission but the beginning. Success is what I do with my failures. Teach me to trust in your love, Lord, and to learn from my mistakes and treacheries.

Wednesday 12th April
Matthew 26:14–25

Then one of the twelve, who was called Judas Iscariot, went to the chief priests and said, "What will you give me if I betray him to you?" They paid him thirty pieces of silver. And from that moment he began to look for an opportunity to betray him. On the first day of Unleavened Bread the disciples came to Jesus, saying, "Where do you want us to make the preparations for you to eat the Passover?" He said, "Go into the city to a certain man, and say to him, 'The Teacher says, My time is near; I will keep the Passover at your house with my disciples.'" So the disciples did as Jesus had directed them, and they prepared the Passover meal. When it was evening, he took his place with the twelve; and while they were eating, he said, "Truly I tell you, one of you will betray me." And they became greatly distressed and began to say to him one after another, "Surely not I, Lord?" He answered, "The one who has dipped his hand into the bowl with me will betray me. The Son of Man goes as it is written of him, but woe to that one by whom the Son of Man is betrayed! It would have been better for that one not to have been born." Judas, who betrayed him, said, "Surely not I, Rabbi?" He replied, "You have said so."

- In some places this day is known as Spy Wednesday. Judas is the spy or sly, sneaky person who secretly approaches the chief priests with the intention of betraying Jesus to them. Jesus uses only words to persuade Judas not to carry out his pact with the chief priests. He takes no other measures to prevent his arrest. What is your reaction to this?

- Like us, Judas didn't see that it is we, not God, who must change. The real sin of Judas was not his betrayal but his rejection of the light. Judas refused to believe in the possibility of forgiveness. Let us not imitate him. No matter what wrong we have done, we can turn to Jesus for forgiveness and healing.

Thursday 13th April
Thursday of Holy Week (Holy Thursday)
John 13:1–15

Now before the festival of the Passover, Jesus knew that his hour had come to depart from this world and go to the Father. Having loved his own who were in the world, he loved them to the end. The devil had already put it into the heart of Judas son of Simon Iscariot to betray him. And during supper Jesus, knowing that the Father had given all things into his hands, and that he had come from God and was going to God, got up from the table, took off his outer robe, and tied a towel around himself. Then he poured water into a basin and began to wash the disciples' feet and to wipe them with the towel that was tied around him. He came to Simon Peter, who said to him, "Lord, are you going to wash my feet?" Jesus answered, "You do not know now what I am doing, but later you will understand." Peter said to him, "You will never wash my feet." Jesus answered, "Unless I wash you, you have no share with me." Simon Peter said to him, "Lord, not my feet only but also my hands and my head!" Jesus said to him, "One who has bathed does not need to wash, except for the feet, but is entirely clean. And you are clean, though not all of you." For he knew who was to betray him; for this reason he said, "Not all of you are clean." After he had washed their feet, had put on his robe, and had returned to the table, he said to them, "Do you know what I have done to you? You call me Teacher and Lord—and you are right, for that is what I am. So if I, your Lord and Teacher, have washed your feet, you also ought to wash one another's feet. For I have set you an example, that you also should do as I have done to you."

- There's much in the Gospel story or words of Jesus that we can't immediately understand. He says little about the meaning of the washing of the feet, except that it's about service, and then just that we should do it too. By doing something in the example or name of Jesus, we often find its meaning.

- I ask to learn what I need to learn from this scene. I note how I feel as I see Jesus rise from table and approach me, kneel before me, and prepare to wash my feet. Help me, Lord, graciously to allow myself to be served and to recognize you in those who care for me.

Friday 14th April
Friday of the Passion of the Lord
(Good Friday)

John 18:1—19:42

. . . So the soldiers, their officer, and the Jewish police arrested Jesus and bound him. . . . Then Pilate entered the headquarters again, summoned Jesus, and asked him, "Are you the King of the Jews?" Jesus answered, "Do you ask this on your own, or did others tell you about me?" Pilate replied, "I am not a Jew, am I? Your own nation and the chief priests have handed you over to me. What have you done?" Jesus answered, "My kingdom is not from this world. If my kingdom were from this world, my followers would be fighting to keep me from being handed over to the Jews. But as it is, my kingdom is not from here." Pilate asked him, "So you are a king?" Jesus answered, "You say that I am a king. For this I was born, and for this I came into the world, to testify to the truth. Everyone who belongs to the truth listens to my voice." Pilate asked him, "What is truth?" After he had said this, he went out to the Jews again and told them, "I find no case against him." . . . Then Pilate took Jesus and had him flogged. . . . And the soldiers wove a crown of thorns and put it on his head, and they dressed him in a purple robe. . . . and carrying the cross by himself, he went out to what is called The Place of the Skull, which in Hebrew is called Golgotha. There they crucified him, and with him two others, one on either side, with Jesus between them. Pilate also had an inscription written and put on the cross. It read, "Jesus of Nazareth, the King of the Jews." . . . After this, when Jesus knew that all was now finished, he said (in order to fulfill the Scripture), "I am thirsty." A jar full of sour wine was standing there. So they put a sponge full of the wine on a branch of hyssop and held it to his mouth. When Jesus had received the wine, he said, "It is finished." Then he bowed his head and gave up his spirit. . . . They took the body of Jesus and wrapped it with the spices in linen cloths, according to the burial custom of the Jews.

- All of us will one day give up our spirit. In prayer we can offer our death to God; we can do so with Mary: "Holy Mary, mother of God, pray for us, sinners; now and at the hour of our death."

- I watch Jesus as he moves through these acts of the Passion: arrest, interrogation, trial, and crucifixion. I observe how he seems calm, and I note the impact he has on others. His sense of vocation, of following the Father's will, never wavers.

Saturday 15th April
Holy Saturday
Matthew 28:1–10

After the sabbath, as the first day of the week was dawning, Mary Magdalene and the other Mary went to see the tomb. And suddenly there was a great earthquake; for an angel of the Lord, descending from heaven, came and rolled back the stone and sat on it. His appearance was like lightning, and his clothing white as snow. For fear of him the guards shook and became like dead men. But the angel said to the women, "Do not be afraid; I know that you are looking for Jesus who was crucified. He is not here; for he has been raised, as he said. Come, see the place where he lay. Then go quickly and tell his disciples, 'He has been raised from the dead, and indeed he is going ahead of you to Galilee; there you will see him.' This is my message for you." So they left the tomb quickly with fear and great joy, and ran to tell his disciples. Suddenly Jesus met them and said, "Greetings!" And they came to him, took hold of his feet, and worshipped him. Then Jesus said to them, "Do not be afraid; go and tell my brothers to go to Galilee; there they will see me."

- The angel and Jesus say to the women, "Do not be afraid." Change, revelation, and enlightenment tempt us to be anxious because we have encountered something so beyond our under-standing. Jesus, help me remember "Do not be afraid" when I sense a transformation beginning in my life.

- Another point in common between the angel and Jesus is that they instructed the women to go tell the other disciples. Our life with Jesus is person-al but not private; the good news is meant to be shared. Am I willing to share this treasure in my life?

Easter
April 16

Something to think and pray about each day this week:

Easter Is a Verb

As author Alice Camille states so well, "Easter is truly a verb, a dynamic event pushing upward from the darkness into the light." Christians are Easter people. What that means to me is that we are dynamic: always growing, changing, moving, and engaging. Even those of us who cannot be "in motion" physically—because of necessary employment, family responsibilities, or health issues—can experience the interior "movements" of the soul. Every day the risen Christ invites us to move, to allow the breaking open that happens in a heart that is open to God and to all that divine love brings to us. We sense the inner movement, we listen to the voice of the Spirit, we pay attention to even fleeting emotions and responses that can be, in God's hands, tools for our ongoing creation.

—Vinita Hampton Wright, from her blog, *Days of Deepening Friendship*

The Presence of God

I pause for a moment and think of the love and the grace that God showers on me: I am created in the image and likeness of God; I am God's dwelling place.

Freedom

Lord, you created me to live in freedom. May your Holy Spirit guide me to follow you freely. Instill in my heart a desire to know and love you more each day.

Consciousness

How am I really feeling? Lighthearted? Heavyhearted?
I may be very much at peace, happy to be here.
Equally, I may be frustrated, worried, or angry.
I acknowledge how I really am. It is the real me that the Lord loves.

The Word

I read the Word of God slowly, a few times over, and I listen to what God is saying to me. (Please turn to the Scripture on the following page. Inspiration points are there should you need them. When you are ready, return here to continue.)

Conversation
I know with certainty there were times when you carried me, Lord. When it was through your strength I got through the dark times in my life.

Conclusion
I thank God for these moments we have spent together and for any insights I have been given concerning the text.

Sunday 16th April
Easter Sunday of the Resurrection of the Lord

John 20:1–9

Early on the first day of the week, while it was still dark, Mary Magdalene came to the tomb and saw that the stone had been removed from the tomb. So she ran and went to Simon Peter and the other disciple, the one whom Jesus loved, and said to them, "They have taken the Lord out of the tomb, and we do not know where they have laid him." Then Peter and the other disciple set out and went toward the tomb. The two were running together, but the other disciple outran Peter and reached the tomb first. He bent down to look in and saw the linen wrappings lying there, but he did not go in. Then Simon Peter came, following him, and went into the tomb. He saw the linen wrappings lying there, and the cloth that had been on Jesus' head, not lying with the linen wrappings but rolled up in a place by itself. Then the other disciple, who reached the tomb first, also went in, and he saw and believed; for as yet they did not understand the Scripture, that he must rise from the dead.

• Neither Peter nor John come to believe in the Resurrection without enduring confusion and uncertainty. But out of the confusion comes clarity.

The empty tomb can only mean that Jesus is truly alive—raised and transformed by the Father. If Jesus is truly risen, then so are we. As we were one with him in his suffering, so are we now one with him in his risen joy. Alleluia!

- Mary went to do her best, to tend to Jesus' mortal remains. She accepted the reality as she saw it but was determined to do what she could to bring dignity and honor. Help us, O God, do what we can as we remain alert, noticing the movement of your Spirit. May we receive life as you offer it to us—even if in unexpected ways.

Suscipe

Take, Lord, and receive all my liberty,
my memory, my understanding,
and my entire will,

all I have and call my own.
You have given all to me.

To you, Lord, I return it.
Everything is yours; do with it what you will.
Give me only your love and your grace;
that is enough for me.

—St. Ignatius of Loyola

Prayer to Know God's Will

May it please the supreme and divine Goodness
To give us all abundant grace
Ever to know his most holy will
And perfectly to fulfill it.

—St. Ignatius of Loyola